LET'S-READ-AND-FIND-OUT SCIENCE®

STAGE 1

How Animal Babies STAY SAFE

by MARY ANN FRASER

HarperCollins*Publishers*

To my parents,
who always kept me safe
—M.A.F.

With special thanks to Robin Dalton
of the Wildlife Conservation Society
for his time and expert review

The *Let's-Read-and-Find-Out Science* book series was originated by Dr. Franklyn M. Branley, Astronomer Emeritus and former Chairman of the American Museum—Hayden Planetarium, and was formerly co-edited by him and Dr. Roma Gans, Professor Emeritus of Childhood Education, Teachers College, Columbia University. Text and illustrations for each of the books in the series are checked for accuracy by an expert in the relevant field. For more information about Let's-Read-and-Find-Out Science books, write to HarperCollins Children's Books, 1350 Avenue of the Americas, New York, NY 10019, or visit our website at www.letsreadandfindout.com.

HarperCollins®, 📖®, and Let's-Read-and-Find-Out Science® are trademarks of HarperCollins Publishers Inc.

Library of Congress Cataloging-in-Publication Data
Fraser, Mary Ann.
   How animal babies stay safe / by Mary Ann Fraser.
     p.   cm.— (Let's-read-and-find-out science. Stage 1)
   ISBN 0-06-028803-5 — ISBN 0-06-028804-3 (lib. bdg.) — ISBN 0-06-445211-5 (pbk.)
   1. Parental behavior in animals—Juvenile literature.   2.   Animals—Infancy—Juvenile literature.
[1. Parental behavior in animals.   2. Animals—Infancy.] I. Title.   II. Series.
QL762.F63   2002   00-057267
591.56'3—dc21

Typography by Elynn Cohen 1 2 3 4 5 6 7 8 9 10 ❖ First Edition

How Animal Babies
STAY SAFE

Many babies can't take care of themselves.
They need an adult to help them stay safe.

Animal parents care for their babies just as your parents care for you. They feed, clean, carry, and protect their young until the babies are old enough to do it for themselves.

Some animal babies may need their parents for a few weeks. Some need them for a few years. Human babies need their parents the longest of all.

There are babies who don't need their parents.

When turtles, snails, snakes, and saltwater crabs hatch, they already know how to find food and escape from their enemies.

This kind of knowledge is called instinct.

Other types of animals are helpless when they are born. They cannot keep themselves warm or get their own food.

Newborn puppies cannot see or walk.

Baby mice are born with no fur.
Their eyes and ears are closed.

Eagle chicks cannot fly until
they have full-grown feathers.

Some animal parents build homes
to keep their young safe and warm.
A nest is such a home. Birds, rats,
rabbits, and squirrels all build nests.

Wolves and bears raise their families in dens.
Chipmunks tunnel into the earth to make burrows.
Each burrow has a special room, or nursery, for the
young.

Animal parents have many ways to move their
young safely from place to place. A leopard cub cannot
run very fast. Its mother lifts it up by the loose skin on
its neck and carries it in her mouth.

Some babies, like young scorpions
or anteaters, ride piggyback.

Young shrews make a train behind
their mother when they travel. They hold
on to one another so none of them gets lost.

There are animals, like kangaroos, that carry their babies in pouches. Inside the warm, cozy pocket the baby kangaroo, or joey, can drink milk and is safe from danger.

A mother alligator sometimes carries her hatchlings in her mouth. No animal would think of going there to snatch one of her young.

Sometimes animal parents must leave their babies behind. These babies often have fur or feathers that blend in with their surroundings. It is harder for their enemies to find them. This is called camouflage.

A fawn, or baby deer, has spots. Its mother leaves the fawn in a clump of plants where the spots help to hide it.

Each kind of animal has a way to alert its young when danger is near.

Monkeys bark or howl.

Ants, bees, and termites use smell.

Fish use motion. Quick fin movements mean "warning."

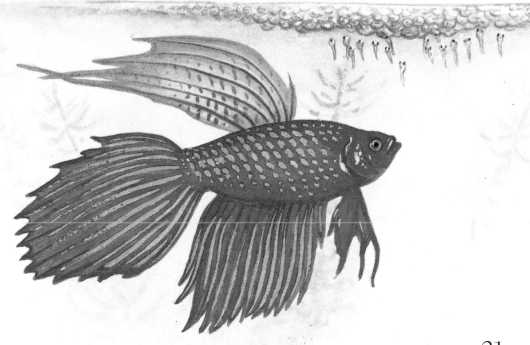

21

When escape is not possible, animal parents will
risk their own lives to protect their children. Hoofed
animals like zebras fight off attackers by kicking and
trampling.

Tigers, wolves, and bears defend
their babies with claws and teeth.

But fighting is risky. Many
animals try to trick their enemies
instead.

A mother raccoon dashes in front of a bobcat to get its attention and then scrambles up another tree. The bobcat chases after the mother and does not find her babies.

Animals that live in groups work together to keep their young safe. Elephants keep their children in the middle of the herd. In this way, all the adults can keep enemies away.

If all the grown-up animals leave to find food, the young must protect one another. Baby penguins will huddle together to form a crèche. By staying together they are less likely to get cold, lost, or eaten.

All kinds of animal babies eventually grow
up and must make their way in the world.

When parents protect and care for their young, their children have a better chance of growing up to have their own children. This is nature's way of helping each kind of animal to survive.

FIND OUT MORE ABOUT ANIMAL BABIES

How Do You Stay Safe?

BEAVER BABIES live in a lodge built by their parents out of logs and branches. The underwater entrance protects them from their enemies. What do you live in, and how does it keep you safe?

A BABY CHIMPANZEE rides on its mother's back so it can stay near her and not get lost. How do you stay near your parents when you go places with them?

A BABY OPOSSUM rides in its mother's pouch for the first ten weeks of life. When you travel in the car, how do you stay safe?

MARA BABIES from several families take care of one another in a single burrow. When your parents must leave, who takes care of you?

MOUNTAIN GOATS snort to warn their young that danger is near. How do your parents warn you about a dangerous situation?

Can you think of some more ways you stay safe?

What to Do If You Find a Baby Animal

Sometimes a baby animal gets separated from its parents. You might find it. But how do you know if it is safe to pick the animal up? It could be sick, or it might bite. Maybe the parents left it there and will return. How do you find out what is best to do?

Here is a list of sources your parents can help you contact for more information.

- A wildlife rescue and rehabilitation organization. For an international listing of such groups and helpful information, try this website: www.tc.umn.edu/~devo0028/
- An animal shelter
- A local veterinarian
- A zoo
- The National Wildlife Federation 8925 Leesburg Pike, Vienna, VA 22184 Telephone: (703) 790-4000 Its website just for kids has interesting information that may help you: www.nwf.org/kids/.